COLORI
CREW

DO YOU SOMETIMES NEED TO SWEAR BUT CAN'T?

DOES IT ANNOY THE SHITAKE MUSHROOM OUT OF YOU?

WELL THEN THIS BOOK IS PERFECT!

EACH PAGE IN THIS BOOK HAS A RELAXING MANDALA CONTAINING A CLEAN SWEAR WORD THAT YOU CAN USE AS OFTEN AS YOU LIKE!

HAPPY COLORING!

ISBN-13: 978-1987431339
ISBN-10: 1987431332

COLORING CREW

WHAT
A LOAD OF
CRUD

COLORING CREW

COTTON
HEADED
NINNY
MUGGINS

COLORING CREW

WOAH
NELLY

COLORING CREW

DARN
IT TO
HECK

COLORING CREW

HOLY
SHATNER

COLORING CREW

YOU
BLINKING
DINGUS

COLORING
CREW

SHUT
YOUR
MEAT
FLAP

COLORING CREW

YOU
STUPID
DOORKNOB

COLORING CREW

WHAT
A LOAD OF
BULLSNOT

COLORING CREW

GO
FRACK
YOURSELF

COLORING CREW

HUSH
YOUR
GOSH DARN
LIPS

COLORING CREW

SON
OF A
MOTHER

COLORING CREW

OH
SHOOTDARN
IT

COLORING CREW

THE
SQUID
HATH
HITTETH
THE
FANETH

COLORING
CREW

FRACKING
HECK

COLORING
CREW

DILL
HEADED
WINKER
TOSS

COLORING
CREW

MOTHER
PUSSBUCKET

COLORING CREW

HOLY
SHITAKE
MUSHROOM

COLORING CREW

WHAT
THE
FUN

COLORING CREW

KISS
MY
FANNY
PACK

COLORING
CREW

COLOR TEST PAGE

COLORING CREW

COLORING CREW

THANKS!
WE HOPE YOU HAD FUN!

IF YOU LIKED THIS BOOK THEN YOU YOU CAN VIEW OUR FULL RANGE OF HILARIOUS ADULT COLORING BOOKS BY GOING TO AMAZON AND SEARCHING FOR “COLORING CREW” AND THEN CLICKING ON OUR AUTHOR PAGE.

THANKS AGAIN!

COLORING CREW

Made in the USA
Las Vegas, NV
02 May 2023

71457047R00026